The Beautiful Truth

Mark Anthony

sometimes words can heal us better than any medicine

LOVE INC. | NEW YORK

Mark Anthony/LOVE INC.
NEW YORK CITY

Publisher's Note: This is a work of fiction. Names, characters, places, and incidents are a product of the author's imagination. Locales and public names are sometimes used for atmospheric purposes. Any resemblance to actual people, living or dead, or to businesses, companies, events, institutions, or locales is completely coincidental.

Book Layout © 2015 BookDesignTemplates.com

The Beautiful Truth/ Mark Anthony. -- 1st ed.
ISBN 978-1-5370295-3-5

To my one and only bird,
the light and love
of my life.

We loved with a love that was more than love.

–EDGAR ALLEN POE

Contents

1.

You have to love her: 24
She was a free spirit: 25
I want to be the one: 26
Most of us need: 27
She has shown me: 28
She wasn't afraid to be herself: 29
I love you in a way: 30
Forgive me: 31
If it doesn't open you: 32
Why do you always: 33
She only showed her silly side: 34
I believe in you: 35
There is somebody out there: 36
She loved the feel of sunlight: 37
Some relationships: 38
When you finally find: 39
Never give up: 40
Sometimes love stays: 41
With so many men: 42
Sometimes when she fell asleep: 43
She didn't care so much for things: 44
You know she's the right one   : 45
Sometimes when I close my eyes: 46
She's worth: 47
She makes me feel: 48
For her: 49
She wasn't afraid: 50
I love all the little things: 51
She was always a little crazy: 52

2.

A strong woman: 55
The ocean taught her: 56
Do you remember: 57
The universe was never something: 58
I fall in love with you constantly: 59
She was a free spirit: 60
Let me love you: 61
Her scars: 62
In the end I needed somebody: 63
Tell me why you love me: 64
Then one day: 65
The beautiful truth is: 66
What is so funny, my dear: 67
When we spoke the other day: 68
I want you: 69
The moon was never as beautiful: 70
You deserve the love you give: 71
I hope that before you go: 72
I want her all the time: 73
I love the way: 74
She sat in a small café: 75
There are so many ways I love her: 76
If I wrote you a book: 77
Reach for me, she said: 78
She loved and lost: 79
She carried with her: 80
She refused to compete: 81

A strong woman: 82

How to explain to you: 83

If you have flaws, my dear: 84

Let me break this down for you: 85

I dreamed we were lost at sea: 86

She was grateful: 87

Once she let go of her past: 88

All the little things about her: 89

I want to tell you: 90

Never doubt: 91

Heartbreak: 92

Sometimes people: 93

Even when she was lonely: 94

I plucked a flower from the sun: 95

I want to share: 96

Our love: 97

She believed in fate: 98

One

Whatever you do, my dear,
you must find a way
to become the hero
of your own story.

Nobody knew
she carried
a secret universe
in her heart,
but those
brave enough
to enter that space
and see
what a beautiful galaxy
her love
could be.

she was reading naked
in the bathtub,
and I don't know what
turned me on more,
her body or her mind.

her smile
is like the sunlight
on the sea. I see tomorrow
in her eyes,
and when she laughs
I feel the universe laugh.

she leaves lipstick prints
on my soul, and tattoos of forever
on my sailor's heart.

I know how lonely it is
waiting to find
the right one;
when everybody else
seems so happy,
but one day
you will look back
and cherish this time
you got to spend alone,
discovering who you are,
before the day you became forever
part of somebody else.

Don't ever stop
being you,
being real,
being what you are,
the spontaneous,
ridiculous, beautiful you;

the you
that doesn't give a shit
what others think
because you are too busy
being yourself.

When I close my eyes
I can remember all of the things
that brought us together,
and when I open them,
I can see all of the reasons
why I am still here.

What she wanted
more than anything
was to be loved
completely
by somebody
with eyes
that saw all of her,
and not just
what they
wanted to see.

She believed
in the kind of love
you can't buy,
the kind you read about
in books.

cherish her,
her magic, her mystery,
her sunshine and rain;

know that she holds
a universe inside of her,
full of many colors,
and places you
will never see.

honor her mystery,
and she will yield to you
the secret heart
of the earth.

Of course you deserve better:
you are everything
and like no one else;
look at how much
you love in secret,
and dream of a better world.

that better world, my dear, is you.

It turns out,
love is not so much
giving her
a bouquet of flowers,
as knowing
when
to hold her like one.

She was far too strong
to let anyone tell her what to do,
so she waited for somebody
who could see
her heart's desire to grow,
and act freely,
who loved her so passionately
and deeply,
she never wanted to be
with anybody else.

She smiled
at the simple things,
reminding me
of their beauty,
and hers.

It took so long
to find you,
yet you came
exactly when
I needed you.

If you are lonely, love,
just remember
there is somebody out there,
just as lonely as you are.

And one day you will meet,
fall in love,
and laugh together
about the days
when you both
were young
and lonely,
and waiting
for each other
to arrive.

Believe in her
and she will bloom
like a flower
into something
so mysterious
and beautiful,
you will wonder
where she came from,
and why
you have been so blessed
to now have her
in your presence.

She designed
her own life,
and was grateful
for just how well
it fit her.

If you want to know the truth,
I've always been in love with her,
even before we met.

I was looking for the light
I find in her eyes,
the grace I see in her walk,
the love I feel in her caring,
her kindness, and her kisses.

Believe in her,
especially when she's down,
especially when she doesn't
have any answers;

Believe in her,
and show her how
you will always be there.

Believe in her,
until she remembers
to believe in herself.

All of her demons
made her stronger
because her angels gave her
the courage to win.

She loved good vibes,
wild waves, warm sun,
kind words, freedom to be herself,
flow, hustle, dreams,
tea, caring, and tacos.

How beautiful a thing
the heart is,
when we have the courage
to show it.

You have to love her
exactly as she is,
not for who
you think
she should be.

She was a free spirit
and a wayward soul,
always in motion
and there were times
when she longed for the sea;

she wasn't perfect,
but perfection never interested her;
she longed instead,
for the sand between her toes,
the sunlight kissing her skin,
the ocean holding her
for a moment,

and letting go.

I want to be the one
you will always look back on,
and not be able to stop yourself
from smiling.

Most of us need
a fucked up relationship
at some point
in our lives,
just so we can learn
what we don't want,
in order to pursue
what we do.

She has shown me
love is a process
of helping each other
grow side-by-side,
and not further apart.

She wasn't afraid
to be herself.

When everybody said,
"be a lamb,"

she showed her fangs
and became a wolf.

I love you in a way
that can't be defined
by a dictionary,
unless it was printed
in the stars,
and each glittering word
expanded into
another galaxy
every time
I said your name.

Forgive me
if I find you beautiful,
but know that I see you
beyond your body,
as I listen to your mind,
and am inspired by your spirit.

For many,
love is only skin deep,
but for me,
that is just the beginning.

if it doesn't open you like a flower,
kiss you like rain
and leave you breathless,
wanting more,
it isn't love.

"why do you always
look at me that way?"

"Like what?"

"You know, smiling
like you do."

"How can I look at you,
and not smile?"

She only showed
her silly side
to those
she found worthy.

I believe in you
the way the sunlight
believes in shadow,
and fishermen
believe in the sea;

I believe in you
as I believe in myself,
as we are one
in the same gospel
sung by the world,
ever since we were young.

There is somebody out there for you,
somebody who will get your soul
and tend to your heart like a flower,
but you must be patient
as the rain
as the sea
as the sky
because finding love
is part of nature,
and will not bloom
until it's season.

she loved the feel of sunlight on her skin,
and fresh flowers in a coffee can;
she loved spontaneous kisses, ice cream,
and getting ready for a night on the town.

she loved deep conversations beneath the stars,
warm salt breezes from the sea,
and the ocean whispering secrets to her,
too beautiful to tell.

Some relationships
are destined to break apart,
so that beneath the shipwrecks
of our broken hearts,
we may find the map
leading us to the one
we will treasure
for a lifetime.

When you finally find
the love of your life,
you will know why
it was worth the wait.

Never give up
on your dreams,
my darling,
for they are
your birthright,
and you owe it
to the world
to become
the Queen,
you are.

Sometimes love stays
and sometimes love goes,
but love always knows,
which way to go.

With so many men
falling at her feet,

she chose the one
still standing.

Sometimes
when she falls asleep on my chest,
I can feel her dreams
bound together with mine
like the pages of a fairy tale.

she didn't care so much for things;
instead, her heart yearned to see new places,
and to meet new people;

she craved new experiences that inspired her
to become greater in spirit,
and to live as freely,
as her heart loved.

you know she's
the right one
when any place
you go
without her,
feels like
the wrong place.

Sometimes
when I close my eyes
I see her so clearly,
I wonder if she is painted
on my very soul.

She's worth
whatever chaos
she brings to the table,
and you know it.

I love all the little things about her
Nobody else knows about,
Like the way she likes to drink her tea,
And get lost in pirate stories.

I love the way she laughs,
And the way her smile reminds me
Of roadside carnivals and boardwalks
Along the seashore of strange towns.

If a man can't see all the little details
That come together to make his woman
Unique in the universe, and love them,

He does not love her.

she makes me feel
the way
only the best art
makes me feel,
as if I'm experiencing
something so beautiful,
and timeless,
I'm humbled
and
grateful to the universe
for her brilliant creation.

for her,
the ocean was a place
of such peace and beauty,
whenever she looked upon it,
she felt as if she was leaving
a bit of her soul behind
as a parting gift,

and that is why
she was always a little sad
to leave, and why
tears have always
reminded her
of the sea.

she wasn't afraid
to run with the wolves,
for she too
was wildly in love
with the moon.

She was always
a little crazy,
which is why
I understand her
so well.

Two

a strong woman
may have suffered,
but heals herself in time,
and her smile reflects
the depth of her experiences,
and is the true source
of her beauty.

a strong woman learns
from her pain,
and knows that feeling
is what makes us
uniquely human.

A strong woman learns
to trust the universe,
and follow her heart
wherever it may take her,
because she knows her strength
will carry her,
and that everything will be okay
in the end.

the ocean taught her
to love,
and let go.

"do you remember
when we first met,
how everything felt
so new and exciting?"

"Yeah."

"I still feel that way,
anytime we laugh,
go the movies,
or find ourselves
walking together
in the rain."

The universe was never
something she feared,
but an endless road
she would travel,
carrying a suitcase
full of flowers,
and a pocket full of promises to herself,
she intended to keep.

I fall in love with you constantly,
the way flowers fall in love
with the rain each day,
slowly,
and inevitably,
the way gravity
lets go of us long enough
to make us believe
we can fly,
then pulls us
back to earth.

She was a free spirit
guided by the wind
and the tide,
and nobody could tell her
how to live.

There was a fire
in her heart,
and passion
in her eyes.

She was like a wild bird
who had never been caged,
and never would be,
and I always love
to watch
her fly.

Let me love you
the way a woman should be loved,
as tender and fiercely
as a wild wind.

Let me devour you with kisses,
poisoned with desire,
and heal you with tender caresses.

Let the earth open its arms
for our love,
and swallow us whole,
for not even death can take away
all of my love for you.

her scars
are a beautiful map
of her past
that lead her
to me.

In the end,
she needed somebody
who understood
her laughter.

"tell me why you love me,"
she said.

"because," he said, "I have
no other choice."

Then one day
she just decided
she would live
for herself,
and not for others
and nobody
had the power
to make her unhappy,
ever again.

the beautiful truth is
I love who I am
when I am with you.

"what is so funny, my dear?"

"you and me,
and how time
doesn't change
how I feel for you."

"do you mean
you love me, then?"

"still, my dear,
and always."

When we spoke the other day,
I didn't know how to tell you
what I wanted to tell you
because the moment
was so perfect,
with us standing together
in sunlight again.

I didn't want to ruin it
with words.

I wanted you
to be the one
I stayed in bed with
on Sunday morning,
and never wanted to leave.

The moon
was never as beautiful
as when I saw it
in your eyes.

You deserve the love you give,
the smiles you bring,
the happiness you share.

You deserve the kisses you leave,
the embraces you gift,
and the life you've always wanted.

I hope that before you go to bed each night
you think back on your day,
and remember something beautiful that happened,
something that made you laugh or smile,
something that reminds you
why this life is worth living;

it is important to remember
all of the little things, my love,
in prayers and in poems,
so that they don't ever disappear.

I want her all the time,
her body
her laughter,
her bright eyes;
I want to lose myself
inside of her world,
and sometimes I don't care
if anybody finds me again.

I want her so much sometimes,
I want to disappear.

I love the way
she moves across the room,
when she doesn't know I'm watching her;
she has a grace and a style
all her own,
and that is what makes her beauty timeless.

She sat in a small café
reading a book of poems,
and everything in the poem
matched everything she felt in her heart,
so that it was a mirror of her soul;

and she loved the twilight
between dreams and the world,
knowing that the moon rises over Paris,
exactly as it does in poems.

There are so many ways I love her:

as tender as the rain
or as fiercely as a storm;

as madly as the moon,
swallowing the sun
or as devoutly as a holy man
on a mountain
braiding clouds of wisdom;

She is like a bird, always moving,
always in flight, and so
I learn to love her
newly each day,
the way the sunlight must
love the earth,
even as it turns away.

If I wrote you a book
in the language of love,
would the words reach your heart,
and lift the veil of sadness
that hides your true face?

And once you saw my words
were only paper and ink,
and that there is only me
to hold you,
would it be enough
for to make you smile,
and remember love,
or would you ask me
to write you
another book?

Reach for me, she said,
not like a lazy lover
who lies on his back
eating grapes, and waiting
for the world to serve him.

Reach for me because you want me,
because you have chosen me
from all the others;
show me
you're willing to work for me
like a simple man
who believes in blood, sweat,
and all the fruits that come
with a hard day's work.

And I promise to yield to you
like the earth,
offering its waist of flowers to the sky.

She loved
and lost,
hurt,
cried,
recovered,
and healed;
she survived,
cried,
then thrived,
and thrived,
and thrived.

She carried
with her
a light,
a spirit,
an energy,
a glow,
that everyone
could feel,
but nobody
could
define.

She refused to compete
with anyone but herself,
and you could always tell
she was winning
by the size of her smile.

A strong woman
will never put up
with your bullshit,
and that is why
you chose her.

How to explain to you
that love isn't what we expect;
it isn't just flowers and moonlight
and kisses, but more quiet, more still,
more constant than the sun;

and all these words
are simply marks in the sand,
waiting for you
to follow them,
until you see the sea.

If you have flaws, my dear,
don't hide them;

For those who truly love you
will see beauty in them,
simply because,
they are part of you.

Let me break this down for you in poetic terms:
she is the Sun, the Moon, and the Stars,
meaning everything, meaning the person
without whom, your life would not be complete;
without whom, you would be just another lonely traveler,
hitchhiking the empty streets at dusk,
still searching for the light in her eyes
to show you the way home.

I dreamed we were lost at sea
on a ship without a name,
but we didn't seem to care,
as we took our turns at the wheel
laughing at our own misguided souls;

as the wind blew through your hair,
and the rain poured down like honey,
I let go of the wheel to hold you in the dark,
and somehow our ship made it back to shore,
where I woke to find you sleeping beside me
with the sunlight still laced in her hair.

she was grateful
for all the world had given her,
and she held unspoken treasures
in her heart,
gifts she gave to others
with a smile,
expecting nothing in return;

her caring was always her finest art,
her greatest gift to the world.

once she let go of her past,
she found herself
flying into a beautiful future
that greeted her with open arms,
as if it had always been
expecting her.

All the little things about her that she sees as flaws,
I consider part of who she is, and beautiful;
and if she could only see what I see,
she'd know there is no such thing as imperfection
when you love somebody completely,
because everything is part of what makes her
who she is, and she the one I adore.

I want to tell you
that when I look at you
I feel an attraction
I can't explain,
as if your body,
your mind,
and your spirit
have already been
imprinted on my soul
as something
so right, so beautiful
and rare,
I can't put it into words,
though God knows,
I'm still trying.

Never doubt
the road you're on
is the one
you're supposed to be on.

The universe picks up everyone,
but only when
we're ready.

Heartbreak
lasts as long
as you need it to,
until you learn how to treat yourself
as well as he should have.

Sometimes people
grow more beautiful
each moment
you speak with them,
as they reveal
their inner beauty,
and spark,
and you can
actually feel
the magic
of their soul,
as it speaks
directly
to yours
in a language
that is as timeless
as it is rare.

Even when she was lonely
there were nights when
she forgot to be sad;
she would find herself
singing some old song on the radio
and it was like the entire world
was now her companion,
as slowly
and surely she remembered
how to feel love
in all the hidden places
inside of her
where she'd forgot to look.

I plucked a flower from the sun
and put in in her hair,
and the radiance of her smile
left shadows on the earth
in the shape of dancing butterflies.

I want to share
the experience
of a strange city with you,
to find all the secret places
where no one can find us.

I want to walk with you,
laughing,
through a foreign rain.

Our love:
Late nights spent together,
talking about nothing,
yet knowing
it's everything.

she believed in fate,
and destiny, and true love,
and that it only happened to you
when you let go,
and lived as if it didn't.

and she lived
happily ever after.

Mark Anthony spent the first half of his life
looking for love,
and the second half of his life
in love with a woman,
who is everything you dream about
in books exactly like this one.

Made in the USA
Middletown, DE
03 November 2016